This self-portrait was painted during the artist's stay at Saint-Rémy; it is a major work for its pictorial lities as well as for the pathos it conveys. Lacking models, Vincent is reduced to painting self-portraits. nething of his inner tragedy shows through in this face aged by suffering. The background and clothes are wn into the general spiralling motion, while the face remains impassive, as though these forces were beyond cent's control. His features are drawn, his mouth pained and the look is absent.

In many ways this portrait is a testament; it brilliantly conveys the end of a dream, the disappointment of ttered hopes and the inevitable tragedy to come

But the seed is sown and his work will grow, feeding on his passions and impulses and translating itself into onstructed shapes and the fulness of colour.

Vincent was a born painter; the spiritual aspirations of his youth were but a form of generosity, of self-denial at the service of an ideal and, perhaps obscurely, a way of appeasing his burning need of giving and receiving love.

But he failed in his allempt at utter self-denial, for his words fell on deaf cars; the soil must be tilled before it can be sown And so what is true for philosophy is also true for men: they are so full of prejudices that they will sooner cling to whatever beliefs they have than open up to new ideas.

Vincent's very first drawings and paintings convey his feelings and emotions in a truthful, poetic and assertive manner.

They will be his way of sowing, endlessly, on whatever ground he chances upon, until the time when, despite or perhaps thanks to all the suffering, his art bursts into bloom in the shape of cypresses, sunflowers and cornfields awaiting to be reaped.

"The House where the Artist was Born", and where he experienced his first child's emotions. He is surrounded by poverty but knows some tenderness. The child develops a capacity for transforming reality.

"The Road at Sunset" brilliantly conveys the enchanting, magical atmosphere of dusk, with the anguish it brings. Everything in this painting is given a romantic and passionate treatment.

The strength and matureness of **"The PotatoDiggers"** and **"The Weaver"** anticipate a personal rhythm and creative force relying on a sound draughtsmanship.

Vincent does not feel the need to look for academic or far-fetched subject-matter: life around him is all he needs. There is no artifice in his approach; he observes, allows his imagination to wander, and transforms the subject before him to suit his very personal vision.

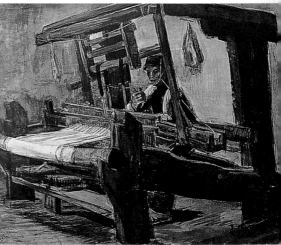

"The Potato-Eaters". Vincent completed this superb painting in 1855 as his father lay dying. In a dimlylit room a family gathers round the table for supper; the tragic, ageless and downcast faces of these poor country people are concentrated on the frugal meal before them.

1885 is an important year for Van Gogh: "The Weavers", a series of solidlyconstructed portraits, **"The Road at Sunset"**, **"The Cross Auction"**, depicting country folk at work, as well as remarkable still lives many of which are based on superb studies and sketches, anticipate the great works to come.

He is back in Nuenen, at his father's, marked for life by what he has seen in the land of peat bogs peopled by poverty-stricken labourers trapped in their wretched lives.Vincent breaks with the past, after his hopeless attempt at being a lay preacher.

He takes up to living a wild, free life, provoking and no doubt rejected by his puritanical environment which either leaves him indifferent or for which he feels downright contempt.

Fitting in no longer, a stranger in his own land, Vincent leaves for Paris, where he will spend two years. In 1888 he makes for Provence. He takes up temporary accommodation in a hotel. It is winter and bitterly cold in Arles. Vincent will paint his first Provençal impressions in his hotel room: the well-known almond flowers in blossom herald the spring and anticipate his most productive period.

Arles, Provence. Vincent arrives at the railway station in the freezing cold and takes up lodgings not far away, in the first hotel he comes across. It is probably the South and the Provençal sunshine that have attracted him to this place. He Ashes to be alone with himself and to express himself freely, far from the influences of Paris. He wants to become a great painter, to *"see another light.. to see that stronger sun"*.

In May Vincent sets up his workshop in the yellow house; for months he had been dreaming of this new-found independence and of welcoming his friend Paul Gauguin, then at Pont-Aven.

"The Yellow House". He writes to Theo : *"Well, today I rented the right wing of that house... it's painted yellow outside, whitewashed inside and well exposed to the sun... "*

Vincent cannot wait for Gauguin to come and join him: *"His coming to join me will alter my way of painting and I shall gain by it...."* After hesitating for months, Gauguin finally arrives there in the autumn; but two months later he is already gone.

"**Vincent's Bedroom**", a soberly-decorated room with the basic furniture of the time and a dash of colour here and there to brighten it up a little.

"**Van Gogh's Chair**", bare, with the inevitable shag tobacco packet; a pleasing harmony of yellows and oranges with a patch of blue.

"**Gauguin's Armchair**" is a more aristocratic seat for the friend whom he admired and felt inferior to.

"The Garden of Aries" . Vincent painted this garden over and over again; it was close to the town cen
and a short distance away from the yellow house. He was constantly searching the neighbourhood for moti
so as not to have to walk too far, and painted a number of gardens and orchards just outside the town.

The trees are treated in a realistic way and their perfume can almost be smelled. The figures in
painting show that the place was visited.

In memory of the painter, the town of Arles has raised a statue to him. It is the work of William E
Singer.

"**The Langlois Bridge**" , named after its owner, spanned the canal leading from Arles to Port-Saint-Bouc. Perhaps it reminded him of the canals of his native Holland. Or was he attracted to the picturesque assemblage of beams supporting the roadway? The subject lent itself to an architectural composition. He works out a colour harmony by combining blues and yellows into a bright symphony. The vertical lines he breaks by means of the water reflections, the inclined rowing boat and the tilted grasses growing in the foreground.

To commemorate the passage of the painter, the regional council of The Bouches-du-Rhône department and the Chamber of Commerce had an identical bridge built on the canal two kilometres away from the town's south-easterly entrance. One of Van Gogh's favourite sites has therefore been brought back to life in the bare, flat land of the Crau.

The Pont Langlois draws strollers, pilgrims and the occasional painter.

"Arles at Night". In this painting Vincent sets out to capture the night-time atmosphere of the sky, with the river mirroring back the town lights.

"The Café at Night", meeting place for night-birds and wanderers, haunt of hangers about and alcoholics. The violent greens, reds and yellows are in sharp contrast with the emptiness of the half-asleep place and its practically deserted tables.

Before leaving for Saint-Rémy, Vincent paints this magnificent view of the hospital garden. Whilst in the hospital, he will also paint the moving scene of patients sitting around a stove in the common room.

It is with some emotion that Vincent leaves Arles, for despite his problems with neighbours, he had inspired pity and won the affection of those who knew him better.

The hospital court has been restored to what it was at the time of Van Gogh. Surrounding it is a cultural complex known as *L'Espace Van Gogh* and made up of exhibition and conference rooms, lecture halls, a public book and record-lending library and small shops.

L'Espace Van Gogh restored to its former glory

From his room at Saint-Rémy, Van Gogh writes: *"I have in my room the Pietà and Delacroix's Good Samaritan"*. He freely interprets these works in his own language. The face of the Virgin is said to resemble that of his mother ...

"The Good Samaritan"; a reminder of the time when he was eager to become a missioner and devote himself to the least fortunate? Once again, a sound draughtsmanship underlies the colour and although these are borrowed themes, they are nonetheless original works of art in their own right.

"The Arles Hospital Common Room" *(see previous page)*

Vincent has this to say about **"The Café at Night, Place du Forum"**: *"It is a night painting with no black, just blue, violet and green"*.

A lantern diffuses abundant light made of pure yellow, and the orange-coloured café pavement seems to detach itself from the night. The night atmosphere is emphasized by the fact that the tables are practically empty and by the few passing figures. The stars pierce the night and the dark street recedes into the unknown in a mysterious perspective which some lit-up windows help to dramatize.

"Portrait of Madame Ginoux" ; Vincent will make several paintings of her. *"At last I have found a woman to sit for me in local costume "*. It will take him one hour to paint the portrait, with *"a pale yellow background, grey face,. black clothes, a black of pure Prussian blue. She leans on a green table and is seated on an orangey wooden chair."*

Vincent had great difficulty in finding models to sit for him; his wild, tramp-like appearance must have put off potential sitters, and those loose women who could have sat for him refused to do so even for a fee lest they be made to look ridiculous in so unconventional a work. Madame Ginoux was the wife of a café owner whose establishment Vincent used to go to with Gauguin who, incidentally, had painted Madame Ginoux before him.

Vincent had been befriended by the Roulin family. Roulin was a jovial, sprightly sort of fellow whom Vincent described as *"a man more interesting than many people ... with a head a little like that of Socrates... adding that he man 1 a thorough Republican and Socialist..."* He will paint the whole family and offer the paintings to them. Roulin will prove a faithful friend throughout the painter's stay at the Arles hospital. In the painting entitled **"The First Steps"**, after Millet, Vincent reveals all the tenderness he could not express otherwise.

"The Man with the Severed Ear" marks a tragic turning point in Vincent's Provençal sojourn. After only a few weeks' communal life with Gauguin, the initial enthusiasm gives way to increasing quarrels which take on a more serious character. Gauguin writes to Theo: *"Vincent and I simply cannot live together due to the fact that we are temperamentally unsuited, and both he and I need peace and quiet for our work"*.

Everything becomes a pretext for confrontation. Van Gogh writes: *"Our discussions are excessively heated and we sometimes come out of them in a state of mental exhaustion"*.

Gauguin had decided to leave the yellow house and Vincent, upset by the failure of his project, was becoming aggressive. On the night of 23rd December as Gauguin was enjoying the Christmas atmosphere out in the streets, he heard coming up behind him the jerky steps he knew all too well. *"I turned round just as Vincent was about to fling himself on me, holding a razor. I must have given him quite an overpowering look for he stopped, lowered his lead, turned back and ran towards the house"*. Gauguin spent the night in a hotel. As for Vincent, no sooner had he reached his bedroom than he cut off the lobe of his right ear. A strong haemorrhage ensued. When the blood eventually ceased to flow, he put his severed lobe inside an envelope, took it to a brothel and handed it to one of the girls, saying: *"Here's something to remember me by."*

All these disturbances had attracted the police, who thought at first that a crime had been committed. Gauguin's arrival on the scene put an end to these suspisions and Vincent was admitted to the general hospital where he was treated for his mental disorders.

During that trying period he was seen to and later befriended by the house doctor on duty, Dr. Rey.

This unfortunate affair will bring wretchedness and loneliness to him and lead to increasing fits.

THE ALYSCAMPS

This row of tombs is what remains of one of the largest necropoles of the Christian world; its finest samples have been scattered throughout the centuries or gathered together in the lapidary museums of Arles. This seat of medieval Christendom, leading up to the church of Saint

Honorat, provided subject matter for the two friends who, each in his own manner, will express their emotion and interpret the rows of ancient tombs lying at the foot of the yellow autumn poplars and alongside a canal.

Vincent, by his we of colour and the introduction of an element of strangeness, leaves the place to its mystery: figures are seen strolling along the path strewn with dead leaves, past the row of sarcophagi cut by the blue vertical poplars.

Gauguin chooses to set his easel up on the canal embankment and direct the spectator's look towards the SaintHonorat church tower; the fiery autumn colours speak out, and three women clad in the traditional Arlesian costume liven up the landscape.

(opposite page)
"The Blue Cart" or "The Market Garden".

Vincent made several drawings, watercolours and oil-paintings of this landscape The painting reproduced here, in Amsterdam's Van Gogh museum, is one of the artist's major works. Everything in this deceptively simple composition is well-balanced, clerverly organized and solidly constructed. The boldly treated foreground adds greater depth to the work, while a perspective is no more than suggested by fences and paths. The distribution of colour produces the most pleasing effect; they are the colours of summer, of harvesting and out-of-door life. The horizon closes in on the hills surrounding the Montmajour abbey in the left hand side of the painting, with the Alpilles behind merging into the background.

Landscapes such as this, serene and gay, reflect Vincent's peace of mind. He is in a state of grace and full of hope. He has asked Gauguin over and knows that he will come. He paints passionate, at the same time loving and well-balanced works. What a long way he has travelled since coming to Arles!

He cannot imagine a more beautiful landscape; he is overjoyed by the light, the colour and what he sees. He can now devote himself to his art and make headway ...

An analysis of Vincent's Provençal period shows a stunning development: during the short time that he painted, he was deeply transformed by his illness but was able to carry the flame of his genius to its apotheosis.

"The Gipsies' Halt"

Despite the small size of the canvas, this is undoubtedly a masterpiece and very representative of the artist's work. In a few bold statements, he says what he has to say.

There is a fulness of colour: the reds, yellows and blues and the sky oscillate in an intense and uncertain light. We can imagine how strong the sun must be just by looking at the figures seeking out the blue shadow. The problem of the foreground being a little Rat is masterfully solved by the placing in the middle of A of an oblique emphasized by perpendicular blades of grass.

In **"The Tarascon Stagecoach"**, where again a sound draughtsmanship is to be found, a subtle play of colour highlights the basic shapes; a strong linear element is present too. The sun, at its height, causes the atmosphere to vibrate.

"The Green Corns". Behind the tilted green corn of the foreground, the field undulates in the wind. In the background, a cypress rises from the centre of the canvas against a background of gently-rolling hills; a *mas* emerges from the folliage.

"The Cornfield" is a festival of pure, violent yet finely harmonized colours; in the distance, under the blue sky, is the white Alpilles chain.

"I loved myself in the imagined splendour of a blondessenced vegetal with sun curls "; this quotation from a poem by R.G. Cadou could well apply to Vincent's state of mind during his stay in Arles.

"The Midday Nap". This very fine work is a free interpretation of an engraving by Millet. The vibrant summer light pervades the ethereal sky and the sun-intoxicated corn. The tender and relaxed attitudes of the resting figures conveys the sluggishness. of midday summer heat whilst the cart in the background adds depth to the painting.

In **"The Haystacks"**, depicting another aspect of the Provençal landscape, a similar range of colours is used, as well as the usual saturated yellow to convey the intensity of light and the strong sun.

"SAINTES-MARIES DE LA MER"

*"Early tomorrow I leave for Sainte[s]
Maries-de-la-Mer on the Mediterranea[n]
coast.. A stagecoach takes you there; it[s]
fifty kilometres away. You cross th[e]
Camargue, grass plains... but mo[st]
important, I am taking with me all I nee[d]
to draw; I must do a lot of drawing.. an[d]
I'd like to come up with something mor[e]
definite and more exaggerated."*

From the Saintes fishing village h[e]
writes to his brother: *"The sea has th[e]
colour of the mackerel, that is, changin[g]
you le not always sure whether it's gree[n]
or violet, you're not always sure wheth[er]
it's blue, for the second after, th[e]
changing reflection has taken [a]
rosegreyish tint... "*. In another letter h[e]
writes: *"On a sandy beach, small gree[n]
red, blue boats with such pretty colou[r]
that you are reminded of flowers... what [I]
wanted to know was how a darker blu[e]
would affect the sky."*

His brief stay at the Saintes-Marie[s]
will reinforce the choice he has made [of]
being a painter of the South, o[f]
exaggerated shapes and colours; thi[s]
journey to land's end, where infinit[y]
opens up before one, will liberate hi[m]
He will come back more sure of himsel[f]
of his calling and confident that he wi[ll]
become a great painter. Vincent paint[ed]
this attractive picture of the village and its solid architecture, and the famous boats " coloured like flowers"
lying on the beach side by side; a simple, yet remarkable work.

"The Sunflowers". There are a number of versions of these astonishing flowers which Vincent may have come across at the foot of the Alpilles, where they are still seen today.

The vineyards was another theme that fascinated Van Gogh. He writes to Theo: *"The vineyards I have just painted are green, crimson, yellow with violet bunches of grapes ... In the vineyard, female figures carrying red umbrellas ... what a symphony of precious colours !..."*

In another letter he writes to his brother Theo: *"On Sunday we saw a red vineyard, all red like red wine, and then the green sky with a sun, and grounds after it had rained, violet and sparkling, yellow here and there where the setting sun reflected itself."*

"The Red Vineyards" is his superb rendering of this.

SAINT-RÉMY DE PROVENCE

After months of convalescence interrupted by frequent crises, a period during which he is often prey to discouragement, he writes to Theo: *"If I did not have your friendship, I should be driven remorselessly to committing suicide and cowardly though I am, I would end up by doing so."*

Unable to extend his stay at Arles hospital, he asks to be admitted to the asylum of Saint-Rémy, on the advice of pastor Salles and backed by Dr. Rey. *"What I should like to do, he writes to Theo, is to go there as an inmate patient at the end of the month or early in May... let's try three months to start with, and we'll see how it goes... it is very likely that I am yet to suffer much. "*

Saint-Rémy is a new chapter in his life, the discovery of new landscapes, the experiencing of a new suffering bringing a renewed inspiration. He discovers the Alpilles, a magical mountain whose hills rise from behind cornfields. On those days he is not well enough to wander out into the country, he paints in the garden. *"The garden with its great pines provides me with plenty of subject-matter; however, the landscape of Saint-Rémy is very attractive and I expect I shall gradually become acquainted with it."* There, he will come across cypresses and olive-trees, irises and sunflowers, cornfields stretching at the foot of he hills... so many potential masterpieces.

Saint-Paul de Mausole
- general view
- inside the asylum
- the enclosing wall

"The Saint-Paul Hospital".

This is arguably one of the finest paintings Van Gogh made of the place. The trees tear themselves from the ground and reach out into the sky in a whirl of branches and colour while the horizontal building in the background helps to emphasize the general movement of this joyful nature.

DOCTOR REY

Early in 1889 Vincent spends a few days in the hospital of Arles, where he is treated by the caring Dr. Rey. To thank him for the care received and in particular for his moral support, Vincent paints the Doctor's portrait (now in St Petersburg's Hermitage Museum) and gives it to him. During his stay there he writes to his brother Theo: "In order to fully reassure you on my account 1 am writing these lines in the study of Dr. Rey, whom you met personally. Now I beg of you one thing hat you do not upset yourself, for it would only add to my worries... "

Returning to Arles from a short absence, during that period of intense agitation, Dr. Rey finds Vincent locked up in the padded cell used M confining the unfortunate lunatics. He has him released from this useless and inhuman ordeal, encouraging him to "eat sufficiently and at regular hours, cut down on coffee and drink less." But Vincent takes little heed of this advice, prey to loneliness and a victim of his passions.

Some months later, following further crises and when Vincent is obliged to leave Arles hospital, Dr. Rey will recommend his patient to the director of the Saint-Paul de Mausole asylum, where the worn-out painter will take refuge.

"Saint-Rémy at Night-Time"

In this painting, perhaps a little out of key with the subject treated, Vincent transposes reality onto another plane, bringing it within the scope of a cosmic vision of things. The message must be conveyed somehow or other and to that end Vincent will not hesitate to use to the full his immense creative powers.

"The Pavement Setters"

The trees and houses can still be seen today. The presence of workers and passers-by helps to liven the work up.

"The Road with the Cypresses"

Central to the work is the tree, vibrating in a cosmos where the stars move about in a brilliant explosion of shape and colour.

"The Reaper" At the foot of the Alpilles and facing the bluish hills that rise to meet the colourless sky, corn undulates in the wind like an ocean of light. Fascinated by colour, Vincent brings out the gold of the fie awaiting to be harvested and breathes life into the landscape. The reaper in the background is drawn into general movement.

"Cornfield with Cypresses" brings together different and oft-treated themes. The wind sweeps all elements along with it in a magical whirling motion and a rhythmic saraband going from sky to foreground.

"The Enclosed Field" is a recurring theme and what Van Gogh saw from his window at Saint-Rémy. But
diversity of energies and marks used, together with the wide range of colours, brings freshness and
ginality to each one of these works, which are a variation on the theme of the closed field.
"The Enclosed Field" and **"The Hills behind the Wall"** represent those territories out of bounds for him on
ount of his poor health. He will breathe life into these landscapes, transforming them and taking his quest
he absolute way beyond the hills and up into the sky.
What is the subject-matter to Vincent, if not a pretext for expressing with utmost urgency that which stems
m his innermost being?

"The Olive-Trees "

Of all the trees, the olive is that which lends itself best to Vincent's tortured brushwork. From the gnarled trunks twisting and winding their painful way up, branches bursting with life and strength and freedom set forth to conquer the space around them, and the rhythm of these spreading branches is beautifully conveyed. The folliage too is drawn into this hectic, all-embracing movement sparing neither hills nor sky.

he Irises"

It is spring-time. River banks and fields are covered in irises that harmoniously blend their green foliage
h the blue-violet of he flowers whose shapes provide compelling painting matter for Vincent's vigorous
shwork.
The painting, sold for a record price at an auction, depicts a profusion of intertwining folliage interspersed
h flowers.

Vincent will make several paintings of irises,
usually bunched-up in vases, blending the green with
the blue and the yellow, symbol of light.

Vincent sows till the very end. His worn out head, where all the passions of men jostle with each other, will know not a moment's respite. Determined to surpass himself, a victim of his passions and suffering from mental disorders, he owes his being alive to the brotherly support of his beloved Theo.

A tragic destiny to which we owe great works filled with pathos.

Van Gogh 's bust in Arles's Jardin d'Été